Preliminary bibliography of the geology and mineral deposits of Nicaragua: USGS Open-File Report 92-547

H. A. Pierce

The BiblioGov Project is an effort to expand awareness of the public documents and records of the U.S. Government via print publications. In broadening the public understanding of government and its work, an enlightened democracy can grow and prosper. Ranging from historic Congressional Bills to the most recent Budget of the United States Government, the BiblioGov Project spans a wealth of government information. These works are now made available through an environmentally friendly, print-on-demand basis, using only what is necessary to meet the required demands of an interested public. We invite you to learn of the records of the U.S. Government, heightening the knowledge and debate that can lead from such publications.

Included are the following Collections:

Budget of The United States Government	Code of Federal Regulations
Presidential Documents	Congressional Documents
United States Code	Economic Indicators
Education Reports from ERIC	Federal Register
GAO Reports	Government Manuals
History of Bills	House Journal
House Rules and Manual	Privacy act Issuances
Public and Private Laws	Statutes at Large

U.S. DEPARTMENT OF THE INTERIOR

U.S. GEOLOGICAL SURVEY

PRELIMINARY BIBLIOGRAPHY OF THE GEOLOGY AND MINERAL

DEPOSITS OF NICARAGUA

by

Herbert A. Pierce

Open-File Report 92-547

U.S. Geological Survey, Center for Inter-American Mineral Resource Investigations, Tucson, Arizona

Introduction

This bibliography was created to gather geoscience references pertinent to mineral deposits, both metallic and non-metallic, in Nicaragua. The U.S. Geological Survey through the Center for Inter-American Mineral Resource Investigations (CIMRI), collects and distributes information for all of South and Central America, as well as the Caribbean and Mexico. Geoscientific research and economic interest in Latin America increase each year, and this list of references should facilitate work by the mineral and geoscience industries.

This bibliography includes references on mines, mineral deposits, seismology, tectonics, paleontology, volcanology, geochemistry, geology, and geophysics in and near Nicaragua. Unpublished literature and theses were included whenever possible. References pertaining to hydrology, botany, zoology, agriculture, or forestry were not included except where these disciplines may be used to supplement information on mineral deposits.

Because many studies cross national borders, several references are regional in scope. These include pertinent works on the Pacific Ocean, Caribbean Sea, Mexico, and northern South America as well as the countries that share a common border with Nicaragua. Studies of the stratigraphy from southern Mexico, Honduras, Costa Rica, Belize, and Guatemala are included because the work that was initiated by oil companies' exploration efforts is more complete. Bathymetry references for both coasts of Nicaragua are included because many structures can be traced using topography to areas well offshore. Geochronology from throughout Central America was included where available to help interpret the timing and emplacement of several features and events related to metallogeny in Nicaragua.

This bibliography is considered preliminary because an exhaustive literature search has not been completed and a number of references, particularly in the "gray" literature, are undoubtedly missing. The bibliography is complete enough that anyone wishing to review the progress of work in the geosciences relating to minerals in Nicaragua should find it a convenient source.

The bibliography was compiled using Papyrus version 6.0.6, then updated to version 7.0. Both versions includes search, group sorts, keyword, and other options for locating items of interest. Some of the references lack page numbers; these references are denoted by (*p.). The bibliography was processed using Microsoft Word version 5.5. Microsoft Word also has search and sort capabilities.

Aburto, Q.R., 1977, The forerunner of "p" waves as an indication of discontinuity in the mantle: Individual Studies by Participants at the International Institute of Seismology and Earthquake Engineering, v. 13, p. 1-11.

Adams, R.H., Dykstra, H., and Salinas, O., 1978, Development and reservoir analysis of Momotombo Geothermal Project, Nicaragua: American Association of Petroleum Geologists Bulletin, v. 62, p. 1207.

--- 1981, Development and reservoir analysis of Momotombo Geothermal Project, Nicaragua: American Association of Petroleum Geologists Studies in Geology, v. 12, p. 27-32.

Adkison, W.L., 1957, Geologic cross sections sponsored by geological societies affiliated or cooperating with American Association of Petroleum Geologists during 1956: American Association of Petroleum Geologists Bulletin, v. 41, p. 1637-1638.

Agency for International Development, 1966, Nicaragua; Inventario nacional de recursos físicos, Centro America y Panama: Managua, Nicaragua, Agency for International Development, Latin America Bureau, * p.

Alcorn, S.R., 1974, Petrogenesis of a Las Lajas Caldera lava and tectonic processes in Nicaragua: Geofisica Internacional, v. 14, p. 67-68.

Allard, P., 1980, Composition isotopique du carbone dans les gaz d'un volcan d'arc; le Momotombo, Nicaragua [Carbon isotope composition of gases from Momotombo, an island arc volcano in Nicaragua]: Comptes Rendus Hebdomadaires des Seances de l'Academie des Sciences Serie D: Sciences Naturelles, v. 290, p. 1525-1528.

Anderson, D.L., 1978, Hot water in underground mining, chap. V in Fernandez-Rubio, R., Benavente, H.R., Lopez, E.A., Pulido, B.A., Tobes, G.M.A., Valle, C.M., and Yangue, B.A., eds., El agua en la mineria y trabajos subterraneos: Granada, Spain, Asociacion Nacional Ingenerios Minas, v. I-III, p. 1111-1123.

Anderson, T.H., and Schmidt, V.A., 1983, The evolution of middle America and the Gulf of Mexico-Caribbean Sea region during Mesozoic time: Geological Society of America Bulletin, v. 94, p. 941-966.

Arden, D.D., Jr., 1975, Geology of Jamaica and the Nicaragua Rise, in Nairn, A.E.M., and Stehli, F.G., eds., The ocean basins and margins; The Gulf of Mexico and the Caribbean: New York, N.Y., Plenum Press, p. 617-661.

Argenal, R., 1977, Nicaragua: Washington, D.C., Publications of the Earth Physics Branch Pan American Institute of Geography and History, v. 46, 182 p.

Ashley, B.E., 1974, The mineral industry of Central America areas, in U.S. Bureau of Mines Mineral Yearbook 1974: Washington, D.C., U.S. Bureau of Mines 1972, v. 3, p. 935-945.

Astorga, G.A., 1987, Paleogeografia Cretacico-Paleogena de las cuencas profundas de Nicaragua meridional y Costa Rica septentrional [Cretaceous-Paleogene paleogeography in the deep basins of central Nicaragua and northern Costa Rica], in Third geologic conference of Costa Rica: San Jose, University of Costa Rica, p. 28.

--- 1988, Geodinamica de las cuencas del Cretacico Superior-Paleogeno de la region "forearc" del sur de Nicaragua y norte de Costa Rica [Geodynamics of the Upper Cretaceous-Paleogene basins of the "forearc" region of southern Nicaragua and northern Costa Rica]: Revista Geologica de America Central, v. 9, p. 1-40.

Babitzke, H.R., and Ashley, B.E., 1976, The mineral industry of Central America areas, in U.S. Bureau of Mines Mineral Yearbook 1976: Washington D.C., U.S. Bureau of Mines, v. 3, p. 993-1015.

Ballard, R.D., 1977, Marine geophysics in the Caribbean: Publications of the Earth Physics Branch Pan American Institute of Geography and History, v. 46, p. 102-104.

Barcelo, G., Cheves, C., Artiles, V., Munoz, A., Boca, D., and Duarte, M., 1989, Investigaciones geológico-geofísicas para petroleo y gas en la region del Pacifico en Nicaragua. [Geological and geophysical investigations for oil and gas in the Pacific region, Nicaragua]: Boletín del Servicio Geológico Nacional de Nicaragua, v. 1, p. 11-15.

Belt, T., and Dana, J.D., 1874, Glacial phenomena in Nicaragua: American Journal of Science, v. 3, p. 594-595.

Belviso, S., Ba, C.N., and Allard, P., 1986, Estimate of carbonyl sulfide (OCS) volcanic source strength deduced from OCS/CO_2 ratios in volcanic gases: Geophysical Research Letters, v. 13, p. 133-136.

Bence, A.E., Papike, J.J., Chandrasekharam, D., Cameron, M., and Camenisch, S., 1973, Petrology of basalts from Leg 15 of the Deep Sea Drilling Project; the central Caribbean: Eos (American Geophysical Union, Transactions), v. 54, p. 995-998.

Bengoechea, A.J., 1959, Arcillas de Las Maderas-Poza del Padre: Boletín del Servicio Geológico Nacional de Nicaragua, v. 3, p. 31-46.

Bengoechéa, A.J., 1963, Distrito Minero del Noreste: Boletín del Servicio Geológico Nacional de Nicaragua, v. 7, p. 13-51.

Bengoechea, G.A., 1961, Los placeres auriferos del area de Quilali, Rio Jicaro, Departamento de Nueva Segovia: Boletín del Servicio Geológico Nacional de Nicaragua, p. 63-99.

Bengston, N.A., 1926, Notes on the physiography of Honduras: Revista Geologica de America Central, v. 16, p. 403-413.

Benhamou, G., Allard, P., Sabroux, J.C., Vitter, G., Dajlevic, D., and Creusot, A., 1988, Oxygen fugacity of gases and rocks from Momotombo Volcano, Nicaragua; application to volcanological monitoring: Journal of Geophysical Research B, v. 93, p. 14,872-14,880.

Bennett, R., and Bennett, C.M., 1972, Exploration and development of geothermal resources in Central America [abs.]: Geological Society of America Abstracts with Programs, v. 4, p. 366.

Benoechéa, A.J., 1963, Distrito Minero del Noreste: Boletín del Servicio Geológico Nacional de Nicaragua, v. 7, p. 13-51.

Bevan, P.A., 1971, La Luz Mines Limited; A summary of exploration for the year, 1970-1971: Managua, Nicaragua, La Luz Mines Limited, 9 p.

--- 1973, Rosita Mine; a brief history and geological description: Canadian Mining and Metallurgical Bulletin, v. 66, p. 80-84.

Bice, D.C., 1979, Tephra correlation and the age of human footprints near Managua, Nicaragua [abs.]: Geological Society of America Abstracts with Programs, v. 11, p. 388.

--- 1980, Eruption rate in Central America estimated from volumes of pumice deposits: Eos (American Geophysical Union, Transactions), v. 61, p. 69.

--- 1980, Tephra stratigraphy and physical aspects of Recent volcanism near Managua, Nicaragua: Berkeley, University of California, Ph.D. dissertation, 476 p.

--- 1980, Origin of Masaya Caldera, Nicaragua [abs.]: Geological Society of America Abstracts with Programs, v. 12, p. 98.

--- 1985, Quaternary volcanic stratigraphy of Managua, Nicaragua; correlation and source assignment for multiple overlapping plinian deposits: Geological Society of America Bulletin, v. 96, p. 533-566.

Bloomer, G., 1974, Paleogeographic evolution of the Caribbean [abs.]: Geological Society of America Abstracts with Programs, v. 6, p. 658-659.

Bock, W.D., 1971, Paleoecology of a section cored on the Nicaragua Rise, Caribbean Sea: Micropaleontology, v. 17, p. 181-196.

--- 1972, The use of foraminifera as indicators of subsidence in the Caribbean, in Transactions of the Caribbean Geologic Conference: Caribbean Geological Conference, v. 6, p. 439-440.

Bohnenberger, O.H., and Dengo, G., 1978, Coal resources in Central America: Geological Society of America Special Papers, v. 179, p. 65-71.

Boletín del Servicio Geológico Nacional de Nicaragua, 1957, Resumen de los reconocimientos de las zonas mineralizadas y otros estudios: Boletín del Servicio Geológico Nacional de Nicaragua, v. 1, p. 5-11.

Boletín Servicio Geológico de Nicaragua, 1958, Resumen de los reconocimientos de zonas mineralizadas: Boletín del Servicio Geológico Nacional de Nicaragua, v. 2, p. 11-16.

Bourgois, J., Azema, J., Baumgartner, P.O., Tournon, J., Desmet, A., and Auboin, J., 1984, The geologic history of the Caribbean-Cocos plate boundary with special reference to the Nicoya Ophiolite Complex (Costa Rica) and D.S.D.P. results (legs 67 and 84 off Guatemala); A synthesis: Tectonophysics, v. 108, p. 1-32.

Braun, L.T., 1971, Geothermal Exploration in Nicaragua, in Proceedings of the symposium on the development and utilization of geothermal resources: New York, N.Y., United Nations, Geothermics Special Issue part 1, no. 2, v. 2, p. 41-42.

Brinton, D.G., 1888, On an ancient human footprint from Nicaragua: American Philosophical Society, v. 24, p. 437-444.

Brown, L., Klein, J., Middleton, R., Sacks, I.S., and Tera, F., 1982, Be(10) in island-arc volcanoes and implications for subduction: Nature, v. 299, p. 718-720.

Brown, R.W., 1947, Fossil plants and human footprints in Nicaragua: Journal of Paleontology, v. 21, p. 38-40.

BULGARGEOMIN, 1982, Objeto rehabilitación de la mina Vesubio, República de Nicaragua: Bulgarian geologic mining service, 66 p.

--- 1982, Oferta Referente al Desagüe, Reconstrucción y Explotación de Pozo Siuna: Corporacíon Nicaraguense de Minas, p. *.

Bullard, F.M., 1956, Volcanic activity in Costa Rica and Nicaragua in 1954: American Geophysical Union Transactions, v. 37, p. 75-82.

Burkart, B., and Self, S., 1985, Extension and rotation of crustal blocks in northern Central America and effect on the volcanic arc: Geology, v. 13, p. 22-26.

Burke, K., Cooper, C., Dewey, J.F., Mann, P., and Pindell, J.L., 1984, Caribbean tectonics and relative plate motions: Geological Society of America Memoir, v. 162, p. 31-63.

Burn, R.G., 1969, The ores of the Pis Pis gold-mining district, N.E. Nicaragua: Leichester, England, Leicester University, Masters thesis, 47 p.

--- 1969, The Pis Pis gold-mining district of N.E. Nicaragua: Mining Magazine, v. 120, p. 169-175.

--- 1971, Localized deformation and recrystallization of sulphides in an epigenetic mineral deposit: Transactions Institute of Mining and Metallurgy, v. 80, p. 116-119.

--- 1971, Localized deformation and recrystallization of sulphides in an epigenetic mineral deposit: Transactions Institute of Mining and Metallurgy, v. 80, no. 774, Sect. B, p. B116-B119.

--- 1973, Geochemical exploration in northeastern Nicaragua: Publicaciones Geológicas del Instituto Centroamericano Investigación Technología Industrial, v. IV, p. 17-29.

Burri, C., and Sonder, R.A., 1934, Ueber vulkanische Gesteine von Nicaragua: Schweizerische Mineralogische und Petrographische Mitteilungen, v. 14, p. 526-527.

--- 1934, Ueber vulkanische Gesteine von Nicaragua: Schweizerische Naturforschende Gesellschaft Verhandlungen, v. 115, p. 325-327.

--- 1936, Beitraege zur Geologie und Petrographie des Jungtertiaeren und Rezenten Vulkanismus in Nicaragua: Zeitschrift Vulkanologie, v. 17, p. 34-92.

Butterlin, J., 1977, Geologie structurale de la region des Caraibes (Mexique; Amerique Centrale; Antilles; Cordillere Caraibe) [Structural geology of the Caribbean region; Mexico, Central America, Antilles, Caribbean mountain range]: Paris, France, Masson, 211 p.

Calderon, A.S., 1882, Los grandes lagos Nicaraguenses (en la America Central): Real Sociedad Espanola de Historia Natural Anales (Madrid), v. 11, p. 193-240, 1 map.

Calvo, V.C., and Bolz, A., 1987, Las calizas de Sapoa y su relacion con el escarpe de Hess, limite septentrional de la plataforma carbonatada de Barra Honda; Costa Rica y Nicaragua [The Sapoa limestones and their relation to the Hess Escarpment, northern edge of the Barra Honda carbonate platform; Costa Rica and Nicaragua], in Proceedings of the Third geologic conference of Costa Rica: San Jose, University of Costa Rica, p. 20.

Capote, M.C., 1984, Experiencias en la utilización de la fotogeología aérea en la busqueda de yacimientos no-metalicos en diferentes sectores de Cuba central [Experiences in using aerial photography for exploration of nonmetallic deposits in various areas of Cuba]: Serie Geológica Centro de Investigaciones Geológicas, v. 6, p. 103-116.

Cardenas, S., and Zoppis, B., 1946, Los yacimentos de tungsteno y molíbdeno de Macuelizo, Nueva Segovia: Boletín del Servicio Geológico Nacional de Nicaragua, v. 5, p. *.

Carr, M.H., Feigenson, M.D., and Bennett, E.A., 1989, Variations of incompatible element and isotopic ratios along the Central American arc; evidence for multiple sources [abs.], chap. Continental magmatism in Proceedings of International Association of Volcanology and Chemistry of the Earth's Interior: Santa Fe, New Mexico, New Mexico Bureau of Mines and Mineral Resources, p. *.

Carr, M.J., 1984, Symmetrical and segmented variation of physical and geochemical characteristics of the Central American volcanic front: Journal of Volcanology and Geothermal Research, v. 20, p. 231-252.

Carr, M.J., Rose, W.I., and Stoiber, R.E., 1982, Central America, in Thorpe, R.S., ed., Andesites; Orogenic andesites and related rocks: New York, John Wiley, p. 149-166.

Carr, M.J., and Stoiber, R.E., 1974, Intermediate depth earthquakes and volcanic eruptions in Central America, 1961-1972: Bulletin of Volcanology, v. 37, p. 326-337.

Carter, T.L., 1910, The gold mining industry in Nicaragua: Engineering and Mining Journal, v. 90, p. 1204-1206.

--- 1910, Mining in Nicaragua: American Institute of Mining Engineers Technical Publications, v. 48, Suppl. B, p. 965-1001.

--- 1911, Nicaragua and its gold industry: Mining and Scientific Press, v. 103, p. 195-199.

Carter, W.D., and Eaton, G.P., 1973, ERTS-1 image contributes to understanding of geologic structures related to Managua earthquake, in Proceedings of the symposium on significant results obtained from the Earth Resources Technology Satellite-1: Washington, D.C., National Aeronautics and Space Administration, Section A, Special Publication 327, v. 1, p. 459-471.

Carter, W.D., and Rinker, J.N., 1976, Structural features related to earthquakes in Managua, Nicaragua, and Cordoba, Mexico, in ERTS-1, a new window on our planet: U.S. Geological Survey, Professional Paper 929, p. 123-125.

Case, J.E., Holcombe, T.L., and Martin, R.G., 1984, Map of geologic provinces in the Caribbean region: Geological Society of America Memoir, v. 162, p. 1-30.

Chamberlin, P.W., 1903, The volcanoes of Nicaragua, in Proceedings of the 57th Congress 2nd session: Washington D.C., U.S. Government Printing Office, Senate Documents 131, p. 27-33.

Chirinos L, M., 1981, Evaluación de los resultados metalúrgicos plantel de Siuna: Corporacíon Nicaraguense de Minas, p. *.

--- 1982, Informe técnico sobre la situación real y futura del planntel de Siuna: Corporacíon Nicaraguense de Minas, p. *.

--- 1982, Estudio preliminar para el tratamiento del mineral alterado (arcilloso) de Siuna por deslamando continuo: Corporacíon Nicaraguense de Minas, p. *.

--- 1982, Evaluación técnica de las operaciones del plantel Siuna Enero-Abril 1982: Corporacíon Nicaraguense de Minas, p. *.

Christofferson, E., 1981, A survey of the Caribbean Sea floor along 82 degrees W for evidence of rifting [abs.]: Geological Society of America Abstracts with Programs, v. 13, p. 426.

Colmet, D.F., 1969, The nature of the clay fraction of volcanic ash soils in the Antilles, Ecuador and Nicaragua, in Panel on volcanic ash soils in Latin America: Turrialba, Interamerican Institute of Agricultural Science, p. B2.1-B2.11.

Combredet, N., and Guilhaumou, N., 1987, Inclusiones fluidas y campos geotérmicos; Estudio de cuarzos hidrotermales en Los Azufres (Mexico) y en Momotombo, Nicaragua [Fluid inclusions and geothermal fields; Hydrothermal quartz study in Los Azufres, Mexico and in Momotombo, Nicaragua]: Geothermia, v. 3, p. 215-227.

Combredet, N., Guilhaumou, N., Cormy, G., and Tiffer, E.M., 1987, Petrographic correlations and analysis of fluid inclusions in hydrothermal quartz crystals from four wells in the Monotombo geothermal field, Nicaragua: Geothermics, v. 16, no. 3, p. 239-254.

Connelly, W.A., 1910, Piz-Piz district, Nicaragua: Mining and Scientific Press, v. 100, p. 350-351.

Cordon, U.J., 1980, Momotombo field models at six stages in time: Transactions of the Geothermal Resources Council, v. 4, p. 443-446.

Cordon, U.J., and Zurfleuh, E.G., 1980, Geophysical investigations at Momotombo, Nicaragua: Transactions of the Geothermal Resources Council, v. 4, p. 447-450.

Crawford, J., 1890, The geological survey of Nicaragua: American Geology, v. 6, p. 377-381.

--- 1891, Viejo Range of Nicaragua: American Geology, v. 8, p. 190.

--- 1891, On the geology of Nicaragua [abs.]: Geologists' Association Proceedings (London), v. 60, p. 812-813.

--- 1892, Notes from a geological survey in Nicaragua [abs.]: Geology Magazine, v. 3, p. 382-383.

--- 1892, The geology of Nicaragua [abs.]: American Association of Petroleum Geologists Bulletin, v. 40, p. 261-270.

--- 1892, The peninsula and volcano of Coseguina: American Association of Petroleum Geologists Bulletin, v. 40, p. 270-274.

--- 1892, Notes from a geological survey in Nicaragua [abs.]: Geological Society of London Abstracts of the Proceedings Quarterly Journal, v. 48, p. 191-192.

--- 1893, Recent discoveries in northeastern Nicaragua; granite hills, moutonned ridges and gold-containing lodes or reefs, and leads or placer mines: Science, v. 22, p. 269-272.

--- 1893, Minerals and resources of northeastern Nicaragua: Bureau of American Republics Monthly Bulletin, v. B, p. 7-17.

--- 1895, Cerro Viejo and its volcanic cones: Proceedings of the Boston Society of Natural History, v. 26, p. 546-557.

Creegan, P.J., 1976, A California structural engineer shares three years of on-site experiences in the design of reparations for buildings in Managua: Jornadas Chilenas de sismología e ingenieria antisísmica, v. 2, p. D1.1-D1.10.

Crenshaw, W.B., Williams, S.N., and Stoiber, R.E., 1982, Fault location by radon and mercury detection at an active volcano; Masaya Caldera complex, Nicaragua: Eos (American Geophysical Union, Transactions), v. 63, p. 1155-1156.

--- 1982, Fault location by radon and mercury detection at an active volcano in Nicaragua: Nature, v. 300, p. 345-346.

Crowe, J.C., and Buffler, R.T., 1986, Multichannel seismic records across the Middle America Trench and Costa Rica-Nicaragua convergent margin, NCY-7 and NIC-1, in Ladd, J.W., and Buffler, R.T., eds., Middle America Trench off Western America: Woods Hole, Woods Hole Marine Science Institute, Regional Atlas Series Ocean Margin Drilling Program, v. 7, p. 11.

Cruden, A., 1989, The Structure of south-western Nicaragua; A preliminary assessment: Luleå, Sweden, Swedish Geologic Co. URAP Map 89001, scale 1:2,500,000. (28 p. Unpublished report.)

Cumming, G.L., Kesler, S.E., and Krstic, D., 1981, Source of lead in Central American and Caribbean mineralization, II. Lead isotope provinces: Earth and Planetary Science Letters, v. 56, p. 199-209.

Darce, M., 1983, Geologia y recursos minerales de las cuencas Rio Viejo-Estero Real y Volcano Pacifico (Porción occidental de República de Nicaragua): México City, Universidad Nacional Autónoma de México, Masters thesis, 143 p.

--- 1987, Geología del distrito minero La Libertad, Nicaragua: Revista Geologica de America Central, v. 7, p. 65-82.

Darce, M., Levi, B., Nyström, J.O., and Tröeng, B., 1989, Alteration patterns in volcanic rocks within an east-west traverse through central Nicaragua: Journal of South American Earth Sciences, v. 2, p. 155-161.

Darce, M., Levi, B., Nystrom, J.O., and Troeng, B., 1988, Alteration in Tertiary volcanic rocks of Nicaragua, and its use as an exploration guide for gold and non-metallic deposits, in Annals of the VII Latin American geologic conference: Belem, Brazil, Sociedade Brasileira de Geologia, v. 7, p. 252-259.

Darce, M., and Rodríguez, N., 1983, Geologia del Area de Bluefields, Zelaya, Nicaragua: Instituto Nicaragüense de Acueductos y Alcantarillados Hojas Geologicas Map 3452 III and 3451 IV, scale 1:50,000.

Darce, R.M., 1985, Aspectos tectónicos de la Region III, Nicaragua [Tectonic aspects of Region III, Nicaragua]: Memorias Congreso Latinoamericano de Geología, v. 6, p. 58-78.

--- 1987, Geologia del distrito minero La Libertad, Nicaragua [Geology of the La Libertad mining district, Nicaragua]: Revista Geológica de América Central, v. 7, p. 65-82.

Darce, R.M., and Rodriguez, V.N., 1979, Riesgos geológicos y volcánicos, Isla de Ometepe (estudio preliminar) [Geologic and volcanic hazards, Ometepe Island (preliminary study)]: Managua, Nicaragua, Instituto de Investigaciones Sismicas, 1-79 p., (1 Map).

DeFilippo, R.J., 1977, The mineral industry of Central American countries, in Area reports; International: U.S. Bureau of Mines, Mines and Mineral Yearbook 1974, v. 3, p. 1079-1097.

De Kalb, C., 1894, The new gold fields of the Mosquito coast of Nicaragua: Engineering and Mining Journal, v. 57, p. 294-295.

Del Guidice, D., 1960, Apuntes sobre la geologia del Departamento de Nueva Segovia: Boletín del Servicio Geológico Nacional de Nicaragua, v. 4, p. 17-37.

--- 1961, Análisis al microscopio polarizador de cortes útiles de rocas provenientes del area de Macuelizo (Nueva Segovia): Boletín del Servicio Geológico Nacional de Nicaragua, v. 5, p. 53-61.

Dengo, G., 1969, Problems of tectonic relations between Central America and the Caribbean: Gulf Coast Association, Geological Society Transactions, v. 19, p. 311-320.

--- 1985, Mid America; Tectonic setting for the Pacific margin from southern Mexico to northwestern Colombia, in Nairn, A.E.M., Churkin, M., Stehli, F.G., and Uyeda, S., eds., The ocean basins and margins: New York, Plenum Press, v. 7A, p. 123-180.

Dengo, G., and Levy, E., 1970, Anotaciones al mapa metalogenetico de America Central: Publicaciones Geológicas del Instituto Centroamericano Investigación Technología Industrial, v. 3, p. 1-15.

Dipippo, R., 1986, Geothermal energy developments in Central America: Bulletin Geothermal Resources Council, v. 15, p. 3-14.

Dobbins, R.J., 1972, Cheilostome Bryozoa of the Northern Mosquito Bank (Nicaragua and Honduras): Baton Rouge, Louisiana State, Masters Thesis, 152 p.

Donnelly, T.W., 1987, Proposal for Caribbean scientific drilling, in Speed, R.C., ed., Caribbean geological evolution; report of a workshop to define Caribbean geological problems, needed investigations, and initiatives for ocean drilling: Evanston, Illinois, Northwest University, Department of Geological Sciences, p. 135-136.

Dovolil, M., 1987, Nerostne suroviny pacificke casti Nikaraguy [Non-metallic substances in the Pacific part of Nicaragua]: Geologicky Pruzkum, v. 29, p. 307-310.

Droxler, A.W., 1987, Cenozoic evolution of small detached carbonate banks and their deep periplatform surroundings in the tectonically active setting of the Nicaragua Rise, in Speed, R.C., ed., Caribbean geological evolution; report of a workshop to define Caribbean geological problems, needed investigations, and initiatives for ocean drilling: Evanston, Illinois, Northwest University, Department of Geology, p. 183-184.

Droxler, A.W., Glaser, K.S., Morse, J.W., and Baker, P.A., 1988, Good agreement between carbonate mineralogical depth variations of surficial periplatform ooze and carbonate saturation levels of the overlying intermediate waters, new data from the Nicaragua Rise: Eos (American Geophysical Union, Transactions), v. 69, p. 1233.

Droxler, A.W., Staples, S.A., Rosencrantz, E., Buffler, R.T., and Baker, P.A., 1988, Origin of Walton Basin by partial tectonic collapse of a large Cenozoic shallow carbonate bank on the northeastern Nicaragua Rise [abs.]: Geological Society of America Abstracts with Programs, v. 20, p. 69.

Echávarri Pérez, A.F., and Gaziola, J.R., 1962, Estudio geológico económico de los yacimentos de tungsteno y molíbdeno de Macuelizo, Nueva Segovia [economic-geologic study of the tungsten and molybdenum deposits of Macuelizo, Nueva Segovia]: Boletín del Servicio Geológico Nacional de Nicaragua, v. 6, p. 23-43.

Eckstein, Y., 1980, Tectonic control of the geothermal resources in Nicaragua, Central America [abs.], in International Geological Congress Abstracts: Paris, International Geological Congress, v. 3, p. 335.

--- 1980, The Momotombo (Nicaragua) geothermal field; transition from a "wet" to a "dry" steam reservoir [abs.]: Geological Society of America Abstracts with Programs, v. 12, p. 419.

--- 1980, New geothermal anomaly in Nicaragua: Geothermal Energy, v. 8, p. 12-20.

--- 1980, New geothermal anomalies in Nicaragua, Central America [abs.], in Abstracts of the 25th International Geologic Congress: Paris, International Geologic Congress, v. 3, p. 1103.

--- 1982, A new geothermal anomaly in Nicaragua: Journal of Hydrology, v. 56, p. 163-174.

Eckstein, Y., and Cik, R., 1982, Use of temperature inversion data for determining the age of fracturing in a geothermal area: Eos (American Geophysical Union, Transactions), v. 63, p. 1091.

Eckstein, Y., Maurath, G., and Ferry, R.A., 1985, Modeling the thermal evolution of an active geothermal system: Journal of Geodynamics, v. 4, p. 149-163.

Ehrenborg, J., in press, The Tertiary volcanism in Nicaragua: Geologiska Föereningen i Stockholm Foerhandlingar, p. *.

Eimon, P.I., 1962, General geology of the Bonanza, Siuna, Rosita areas, Nicaragua:, 15 p.

Elming, S.A., 1985, A paleomagnetic investigation and K-Ar age determinations of volcanic rocks in Nicaragua: Luleå, Sweden and Managua, Nicaragua, Instituto Nicaragüense de Acueductos y Alcantarillados, 37 p.

Emmet, P.A., 1983, Montana de Comayagua structural belt; Neogene rejuvenation of a Laramide wrench fault as a dextral transform to the Honduras Depression [abs.]: Geological Society of America Abstracts with Programs, v. 15, p. 567.

Engels, B., 1965, Geologische problematik und strukturanalyse Nikaraguas (Ein Beitrag zur Geologie Mittelamerikas): Geologische Rundschau, v. 54, p. 758-795.

--- 1967, Zur Geologie von Chile und Nicaragua [Geology of Chile and Nicaragua]: Deutsche Geologische Gesellschaft Zeitschrift [Hannover], v. 116, p. 974-975.

Engels, P.B., 1964, Resumen del estudio geológico sobre la tectónica interna de la región esquistosa de Nueva Segovia, Nicaragua: Boletín del Servicio Geológico Nacional de Nicaragua, v. 8, p. 11-52.

Entwistle, L.P., 1975, Neptune Mining Company, Bonanza, Nicaragua; an appraisal of the future: Managua, Nicaragua, Neptune Mining Co., * p.

Ernest K. Lehmann and Associates, Inc., 1984, Reporte final de los estudios de exploración minera en Nicaragua: Corporacíon Nicaraguense de Minas, v. 1, no. 2, part D, p. 96.

Espinosa, A.F., 1983, Nicaragua: U.S. Geological Survey Professional Paper 285, 52 p.

Eswaran, H., 1972, Micromorphological indicators of pedogenesis in some tropical soils derived from basalts from Nicaragua: Geoderma, v. 7, p. 15-31.

Eswaran, H., and De Coninck, F., 1971, Clay mineral formations and transformations in basaltic soils in tropical environments: Pedologie, v. 21, p. 181-210.

Eswaran, H., and Sys, C., 1970, An evolution of the free iron in tropical basaltic soils: Pedologie, v. 20, p. 62-85.

Falconbridge Nickel Mines Ltd., 1964-1970, Annual Reports; Falconbridge Nickel Mines Ltd: Falconbridge Nickel Mines Ltd., * p.

Feigenson, M.D., Carr, M.J., and Walker, J.A., 1985, Geochemically distinct sources for interstratified lavas from the Nejapa cinder cone alignment, Nicaragua [abs.]: Geological Society of America Abstracts with Programs, v. 17, p. 580.

Ferrari, B., and Viramonte, J., 1973, Contribución al conocimiento de la geomorfología regional de Nicaragua [Contribution to the understanding of the regional geomorphology of Nicaragua]: Publicaciones Geológicas del Instituto Centroamericano Investigación Technología Industrial, v. 4, p. 96-103.

Ferrey, O.C., 1974, Cano Chacalín, Nicaragua: Servicio Geológico Nacional de Nicaragua Mapa Geológico Map 3358-3, scale 1:50,000.

--- 1975, Río Agua Zarca, Nicaragua: Servicio Geológico Nacional de Nicaragua Mapa Geológico Map 3358-2, scale 1:50,000.

Feust, A., 1912, The Chontales mining district, Nicaragua: Mining and Scientific Press, v. 105, p. 720-722.

Figge, K., 1966, Die stratigraphische Stellung der metamorphen Gesteine NW-Nicaraguas: Neues Jahrbuch für Geologie und Paläontologie. Monatshefte, v. 4, p. 234-247.

Flaherty, G.F., 1960, Geological Report, La Luz Mines Ltd., Nicaragua, C.A: La Luz Mines Ltd., 31 p.

Flaherty, G.F., Mackay, J.M., and Mustard, G.W., 1959, A study of Rosita Mines Ltd: Rosita Mines, * p.

Garayar, J., and Martinez, N.P., 1973, El Castillo, Nicaragua; Costa Rica: Servicio Geológico Nacional de Nicaragua Mapa Geológico Map 3349-2, scale 1:50,000.

Garayar, S.J., and Viramonte, J., 1973, Hallazgo de peridotitas en Nicaragua [Discovery of peridotite in Nicaragua]: Publicaciones Geológicas del Instituto Centroamericano Investigación Technología Industrial, v. 4, p. 105-114.

Garbrech, L., 1920, New mining field in eastern Nicaragua: Engineering and Mining Journal, v. 109, p. 791-797.

Garbrecht, L., 1920, New mining fields in eastern Nicaragua: Engineering and Mining Journal, v. 109, p. 791-797.

Garzón, M., Cruz, L.M., Sinclair, A., Castellón, R., Doran, J., and Darce, M., 1991, Exploración geológica del yacimento Foundling, flancos SW-NE: Corporación Nicaraguense de Minas, p. 8.

Gemmell, B., 1982, Metallic trace elements in Central American fumarolic condensates: Eos (American Geophysical Union, Transactions), v. 63, p. 1153.

Gemmell, J.B., 1987, Geochemistry of metallic trace elements in fumarolic condensates from Nicaraguan and Costa Rican volcanoes: Journal of Volcanology and Geothermal Research, v. 33, p. 161-181.

GEONIC, 1990, Informe final; Exploración geológica Neblina Flanco S-W: Corporacíon Nicaraguense de Minas, p. 7.

Gerbrecht, L., 1920, New mining fields in northeastern Nicaragua: Engineering and Mining Journal, v. 109, p. 791-797.

del Giudice, D., 1959, Notas preliminares sobre el oro y la plata en Murra (Nueva Segovia): Boletín del Servicio Geológico Nacional de Nicaragua, v. 3, p. 17-19.

--- 1959, Informe sobre las investigaciones de las "fuerzas endógenas" en Nicaragua: Boletín del Servicio Geológico Nacional de Nicaragua, v. 3, p. 51-84.

Gleason, R.J., 1977, Wall-rock alteration, fluid inclusion, and mine water analyses of the Panteon vein system, Limón, Nicaragua: Hanover, New Hampshire, Dartmouth College, Masters Thesis, 105 p.

--- 1980, Wall-rock alteration around the Panteon vein system; Limon mining district, Nicaragua [abs.]: Geological Society of America Abstracts with Programs, v. 12, p. 434.

Goldsmith, L.H., 1980, Regional and local geologic structure of the Momotombo Field, Nicaragua: Transactions of the Geothermal Resources Council, v. 4, p. 125-128.

Gombert, D.N., Banks, P.O., and McBirney, A.R., 1968, Guatemala; Preliminary zircon ages from Central Cordillera: Science, v. 162, p. 121-122.

Gonfiantini, R., 1984, Latin America; isotopes to tap Earth's thermal energy: International Atomic Energy Agency Bulletin, v. 26, p. 45-46.

Gose, W.A., 1980, Evidence for a tectonic discontinuity in Nicaragua: Eos (American Geophysical Union, Transactions), v. 61, p. 946.

--- 1983, Late Cretaceous-early Tertiary tectonic history of southern Central America: Journal of Geophysical Research B, v. 88, p. 10585-10592.

--- 1985, Tectonic implications of paleomagnetic data from Caribbean: Earthquake Notes, v. 55, p. 28.

Gose, W.A., Scott, G.R., and Swartz, D.K., 1980, The aggregation of mesoamerica; paleomagnetic evidence, in Pilger, R.H., Jr., ed., Proceedings of a symposium on the origin of the Gulf of Mexico and the early opening of the central North Atlantic: Baton Rouge, Louisiana, Louisiana State University, p. 51-54.

Gottschalk, A.L.M., 1903, Gold fields of eastern Nicaragua, in : Daily Consular Reports 1774, p. 2-9.

Gough, D.I., and Heirtzler, J.R., 1969, Magnetic anomalies and tectonics of the Cayman Trough: Royal Astronomical Society Geophysical Journal, v. 18, p. 33-49.

Griffin, J.B., 1956, The reliability of radiocarbon dates for late glacial and recent times in central and eastern North America, in Papers of the 3d Great Basin Archeological Conference: Salt Lake City, Utah, University of Utah, p. 10-34.

Grose, L.T., 1974, Geothermal: Geotimes, v. 19, p. 20-21.

Guendel, F., and McNally, K.C., 1986, High resolution evidence of smooth Benioff zone gradations approaching the southern terminus of the Middle America Trench: Eos (American Geophysical Union, Transactions), v. 67, p. 1114.

Guffanti, M., 1984, Worldwide; Geothermal power continues to grow: Geotimes, v. 29, p. 12-13.

Hålenius, U., 1985, Fluid inclusion microthermetry on quartz from the Panteón vein, El Limón area, Nicaragua: Luleå, Sweden, Instituto Nicaragua de Minas (INMINE), 30 p.

Hallock, P., Hine, A.C., Vargo, G.A., Elrod, J.A., and Jaap, W.C., 1988, Platforms of the Nicaraguan Rise; examples of the sensitivity of carbonate sedimentation to excess tropic resources: Geology, v. 16, p. 1104-1107.

Hallock, P., Vargo, G.A., Hine, A.C., Triffleman, N.J., Boomer, K.J., Jaap, W.C., and Belknap, D.F., 1987, Platforms of the Nicaraguan Rise; examples of suppression of carbonate accumulation by excess nutrients? [abs.]: Geological Society of America Abstracts with Programs, v. 19, p. 691.

Harlow, D.H., White, R.A., and Aburto, Q.A., 1980, Shallow seismicity in western Nicaragua: Eos (American Geophysical Union, Transactions), v. 61, p. 1028.

Harlow, D.H., White, R.A., Cifuentes, I.L., and Aburto, Q.A., 1981, Quiet zone within a seismic gap near western Nicaragua; possible location of a future large earthquake: Science, v. 213, p. 648-651.

Harthill, N., and Keller, G.V., 1971, Some aspects of the megatectonics of northern Central America: Eos (American Geophysical Union, Transactions), v. 52, p. 351.

Hawxhurst, R., Jr., 1921, The Piz Piz gold district, Nicaragua: Mining and Scientific Press, v. 122, p. 353-360.

Hazlett, R.W., 1981, Structural controls on Quaternary volcanism, northwestern Nicaragua [abs.]: Geological Society of America Abstracts with Programs, v. 13, p. 60.

— 1987, Geology of the San Cristobal volcanic complex, Nicaragua: Journal of Volcanology and Geothermal Research, v. 33, p. 223-230.

Heiken, G., and Wohletz, K., 1985, Volcanic ash: Berkeley, California, University of California Press, Los Alamos Series in Basic and Applied Sciences, * p.

Heim, A., 1926, Vulkanische Ereignisse; Berichte ueber die juengste vulkanische Taetigkeit in Mittelamerika: Zeitschrift Vulkanologie, v. 10, p. 114-119.

Helbig, K., 1967, Nicaragua--Land der Seen und Volkane: Kosmos, v. 63, p. 205-210.

Hernandez, A., 1977, Orientation of Managua's faults, in Proceedings of the 6th World Conference on Earthquake Engineering: New Delhi, World Conference Earthquake Engineering, v. 6, p. 304-307.

Hershey, O.H., 1912, Geological reconnaissance in northeastern Nicaragua: Geological Society of America Bulletin, v. 23, p. 493-516.

--- 1912, Geology of the Pis Pis mining district in Nicaragua: Mining and Scientific Press, v. 194, p. 270-272.

Hesselbom, A., 1982, Reporte de una Investigación Magnetométrica en el Area de Cerro Güergüero, Siuna, Nicaragua: Sverges Geologiska A.B., 2 p.

--- 1985, Geophysical methods in the exploration for gold-bearing quartz veins in Nicaragua: Geoexploration, v. 23, p. 416-417.

Hine, A.C., and Hallock, P., 1987, Carbonate platforms of the Nicaraguan Rise; overview [abs.]: Geological Society of America Abstracts with Programs, v. 19, p. 703.

Hine, A.C., Harris, M.W., Hallock, P., Mullins, H.T., Belknap, D.F., and Neumann, A.C., 1988, Structure, stratigraphy, and sedimentation of a current-dominated open seaway within a carbonate platform complex; Miskito Channel, Nicaraguan Rise, SW Caribbean Sea [abs.]: Geological Society of America Abstracts with Programs, v. 20, p. 70.

Hobbs, W.H., 1944, New volcanoes and a new mountain range [Mexico]: Science, v. 99, p. 287-290.

Hodgson, G., 1985, Geología de un area de la provincia central este de Nicaragua: Managua, Nicaragua, Instituto Nicaragüense de Estudios Territoriales, 82 p.

Hodgson, G., Troeng, D., and Rodrigues, D., 1988, Geology of the Rincon de Garcia gold deposit, Nicaragua: Congresso Latino Americano de Geología, v. 7, p. 113-126.

Hodgson, V.G., 1972, El Aparejo, Nicaragua: Servicio Geológico Nacional de Nicaragua Mapa Geologico Map 3250-1, scale 1:50,000.

--- 1972, El Almendro, Nicaragua: Servico Geológico Nacional de Nicaragua Mapa Geológico Map 3251-2, scale 1:50,000.

--- 1974, Atlanta, Nicaragua: Servicio Geológico Nacional de Nicaragua Mapa Geológico Map 3350-1, scale 1:50,000.

--- 1974, Rio El Almacen, Nicaragua: Servicio Geológico Nacional de Nicaragua Mapa Geológico Map 3350-4, scale 1:50,000.

--- 1974, Barra del Rio Maiz, Nicaragua [The bars of Rio Maiz, Nicaragua]: Servicio Geológico Nacional de Nicaragua Mapa Geológico Map 3449-4, scale 1:50,000.

--- 1974, Monkey Point, Nicaragua: Servicio Geológico, Managua, Nicaragua Mapa Geologíco Map 3450-1, scale 1:50,000.

--- 1974, Rio Pijibaye, Nicaragua: Servicio Geológico Nacional de Nicaragua Mapa Geológico Map 3450-3, scale 1:50,000.

--- 1974, Punta Gorda, Nicaragua: Servico Geológico Nacional de Nicaragua Mapa Geológico Map 3450-4, scale 1:50,000.

Hoffstetter, R., Dengo, G.O., and Weyl, R., 1960, Costa Rica: Recherche Sciences, p. 225-306.

Hoffstetter, R., Zoppis, B.L., and Dengo, G.O., 1960, Nicaragua: Recherche Sciences, p. 171-224.

Holcombe, T.L., 1974, Late Cretaceous and Cenozoic sedimentary strata of the Caribbean [abs.]: Geological Society of America Abstracts with Programs, v. 6, p. 798-799.

Honkala, F.S., 1955, Selected bibliography of standard stratigraphic sections of North America: Geological Society of America Bulletin, v. 66, p. 153-154.

Houston, M.H., Jr., and Shaub, F.J., 1977, Middle America Trench; Nicaragua: Eos (American Geophysical Union, Transactions), v. 58, p. 1150.

Hoylman, H.W., and Chilingar, G.V., 1965, Geología petrolera y exploracíon en Nicaragua: Boletín de Asociacíon Mexicana Geólogos Petroleros, v. 17, p. 1-16.

Imlay, R.W., 1952, Correlation of the Jurassic formations of North America, exclusive of Canada: Geological Society of America Bulletin, v. 63, p. 953-992.

INMINE, 1983, Estadisticas del plantel Siuna: Corporacíon Nicaraguense de Minas, p. *.

--- 1986, Mina Vesubio, Cálculo de reservas al 01-08-1986: Corporacíon Nicaraguense de Minas, p. *.

--- 1987, Informe del estado y perspectivas de desarrollo de la industria aurifera en el Complejo Minero Bonanza: Corporacíon Nicaraguense de Minas, p. *.

--- 1987, Descripción del plantel de oro, Bonanza: Corporacíon Nicaraguense de Minas, p. *.

--- 1988, Proyecto conceptual de viabilidad en la explotación Tajo abierto - Siuna: Corporacíon Nicaraguense de Minas, p. *.

--- 1989, Plan integral de desarrollo, Empressa Minera Bonanza, 1989-1991: Corporacíon Nicaraguense de Minas, p. 80.

--- 1989, Situación general Empresa Minera Siuna (Alcaldía Municipal de Siuna): Corporacíon Nicaraguense de Minas, p. *.

--- 1991, Informe geológico y reservas calculadas del depósito de Neblina: Corporacíon Nicaraguense de Minas, p. *.

--- 1991, Informe sobre plan de mantenimento del plantel de empresa minera Bonanza: Corporacíon Nicaraguense de Minas, p. *.

--- 1991, Empresa minera Bonanza, S.A. costos de operación, mantenimento del molino: Corporacíon Nicaraguense de Minas, p. *.

--- 1991, Empresa minera Bonanza, S.A. informe semestral Dirección de Metalurgia: Corporacíon Nicaraguense de Minas, p. *.

INMINE-SGAB, 1989, Evaluación del potencial para el desarrollo productivo en la Empresa Minera Siuna: Coporación Nicaraguense de Minas and Sverges Geologiska A.B., 23 p.

Jiranek, J., 1983, Composición y propiedades de tierras blancas Nicaragüenses; posibilidades del beneficio y el uso potencial de zeolitas: Managua, Instituto Nicaragüense de la Minería, 45 p.

--- 1988, Hydrothermal kaolinization of andesites in Mombacho Volcano, Nicaragua, in Konta, J., ed., Proceedings of the 10th Conference on Clay Mineralogy and Petrology: Ostrava, Sweden, p. 323-327.

Joannesson, T., Castellón, R., Dornan, J., Sinclair, A., and Darce, M., 1991, Cálculo de reservas auriferas de la estructura Atlas I, Bonanza: Corporación Nicaraguense de Minas, 21 p.

Johannesson, T., Castellón, R., Doran, J., Sinclair, A., and Darce, M., 1991, Cálculo de reservas auriferas de la estructura Atlas I, Bonanza: Corporacíon Nicaraguense de Minas, p. 21, unpublished report.

Karim, M.F., 1965, Some geochemical methods of prospecting and exploration for oil and gas: Dissertation Abstracts, v. 25, p. 5168.

Karim, M.F., and Chilingar, G., 1964, Estudio geoquímico de la Costa del Atlantico de Nicaragua: Boletín del Servicio Geológico Nacional de Nicaragua, v. 8, p. 109-121.

Karim, M.F., and Chilingar, G.V., 1963, Exploración geoquímica para petroleo en la Costa del Pacifico de Nicaragua: Boletín del Servicio Geológico Nacional de Nicaragua, v. 7, p. 97-136.

--- 1964, Nicaragua's Pacific coast has oil possibilities: World Oil, v. 159, p. 117-124.

Kay, G.M., 1951, North American geosynclines: Geological Society of America Memoir, v. 48, p. 143.

Kesler, S.E., 1971, Nature of ancestral orogenic zone in nuclear Central America: American Association of Petroleum Geologists Bulletin, v. 55, p. 2116-2129.

King, P.B., 1951, The tectonics of middle North America--Middle North America east of the Cordilleran system: Princeton, N.J., Princeton University Press, 203 p.

Klonsky, L.F., 1977, A preliminary study of the origin of the physiographic boundary between the Nicaraguan Rise and Colombian Basin, Caribbean Sea: New Brunswick, Rutgers State University, Masters thesis, 115 p.

Knackey, M.J., 1979, Report of exploration by La Luz Mines Ltd. for the fiscal year of 1969-1979: La Luz Mines, * p.

Kondakov, L.A., and Nabrovenkov, O.S., 1982, Nekotoryye cherti geologicheskogo stroyeniya Nikaragua [Some traits of the geologic structure of Nicaragua]: Izvestiya Akademii Nauk SSSR. Seriya Geologicheskaya, v. 7, p. 114-122.

--- 1983, Osnovnyye cherti metallogenii Nikaragua [Principal characteristics of metallogeny in Nicaragua]: Izvestiya Akademii Nauk SSSR. Seriya Geologicheskaya, v. 3, p. 91-104.

Kruckow, T., 1982, Some aspects of the development of Paleocaribbean molluscan faunas: Brenesia, v. 19-20, p. 353-357.

Krusi, A., and Shultz, J., 1979, Base surge deposits of the Nicaraguan volcano Masaya [abs.]: Geological Society of America Abstracts with Programs, v. 11, p. 87-88.

Lagana, T., 1957, Interpretación geofísica del estudio efectuado en Palacagüina: Boletín del Servicio Geológico Nacional de Nicaragua, v. 1, p. 35-37.

--- 1960, El Tungsteno y el Molíbdeno de Macuelizo: Boletín del Servicio Geológico Nacional de Nicaragua, p. 13-16.

Laguna, M.J.E., 1987, División geotectónica de Centroamérica y el sistema de falla Murciélago-Hess, in Proceedings of the Third Geologic Conference of Costa Rica: San Jose, University of Costa Rica, p. 34.

Lamb, H.J., 1974, The use of multiple regression methods in predicting the gold values in Mina Panteon, El Limon, Nicaragua; an epithermal gold-silver vein type deposit: Houghton, Michigan Technological University, Masters thesis, 52 p.

Langmuir, C.H., Goldstein, S., Zindler, A., Weaver, S., Staudigel, H., Carr, M., and Walker, J., 1981, Nd and Sr isotopic composition of Central American volcanos: Eos (American Geophysical Union, Transactions), v. 62, p. 440.

Langohr, R., 1974 [1975], Transport en afzetting van vulkanische assen in Centraal-Chili, Italiee, Nicaragua en Java [Transport and deposition of volcanic ashes in central Chile, Italy, Nicaragua, and Java]: Natuurwetenschappelijk Tijdschrift [Ghent], v. 56, p. 27-44, 29 refs.

Lara, I., Dominquez, A.C., and Bermúdez, F., 1989, Proyecto de Desarrollo del Tajo Abierto en la Empresa Minera Siuna: Universidad Nacional de Ingerieria, Managua, Nicaragua, Ingeniero degree, * p.

Lefebure, D.V., 1986, The mina El Limón area and the Telica complex; two examples of Cenozoic volcanism in northwestern Nicaragua, Central America: Ottawa, Ontario, Carleton University, Ph.D. dissertation, 190 p.

Lefebure, D.V., and Bell, K., 1978, Two areas of Cenozoic volcanism in northwestern Nicaragua [abs.]: Geological Society of America Abstracts with Programs, v. 10, p. 442.

Lehmann, E.K., 1984, Reporte final de los estudios de exploración minera en Nicaragua: Corporacíon Nicaraguense de Minas, part c, p. 113.

Levi, B., Nystrom, J.O., Darce, M., and Troeng, B., 1987, Alteration Patterns in volcanic rocks from a geotraverse through Nicaragua: Luleå, Sweden, Sverges Geologiska A.B., 27 p.

Levy, E., 1964, Rasgos geologicos del intrusivo de San Juan de Telpaneca: Boletín del Servicio Geológico Nacional de Nicaragua, v. 8, p. 53-67.

--- 1966, Exploracion geoquimica en Nicaragua: Publicaciones Geológicas del Instituto Centroamericano Investigación Technología Industrial, v. 1, p. 1-3.

Lilljequist, R., 1984, Investigations of hydrothermal alteration zones in the Limón district, Nicaragua: Luleå, Sweden, Sverges Geologiska A.B., 27 p.

Lilljequist, R., Andersson, L.C., and Aastrand, P., 1984, Megastructures in Cenozoic volcanics in Nicaragua, Central America, and their relation to mineral deposits, in Morris-Jones, D.R., and Cook, J.J., eds., Proceedings of the International Symposium on Remote Sensing of Environment: Remote sensing for exploration geology Third thematic conference, v. 1, p. *.

Lopez, C.A., 1982, Thermal structure and hydrogeochemistry of the Momotombo geothermal field, Nicaragua, C.A: Kent, Ohio, Kent State University, Masters thesis, 174 p.

Lopez, C.V., and Eckstein, Y., 1980, Six month production test at Momotombo, Nicaragua; preliminary results: Transactions of the Geothermal Resources Council, v. 4, p. 357-360.

Lopez, C.V., Hoyt, B.R., and Eckstein, Y., 1980, Subsurface temperature distribution and structure of the geothermal reservoir at Momotombo, Nicaragua: Transactions of the Geothermal Resources Council, v. 4, p. 459-462.

Lopez, V.C., 1977, Analysis and interpretation of waters and gases of the Momotombo Field, Nicaragua: Geothermal Energy, v. 5, p. 14-17.

--- 1978, Discussion of the hydrogeochemistry of the El Joyo-Obraje Valley and the possible relation with the Momotombo geothermal field at Nicaragua: Geothermal Energy, v. 6, p. 7-12.

MacDonald, W.D., 1978, Domains of tectonic rotation; paleomagnetic evidence from the western Caribbean: Eos (American Geophysical Union, Transactions), v. 59, p. 271.

MacKenzie, L.R., 1974, preliminary Studies, Siuna, Nicaragua: La Luz Mines Ltd., * p.

Maher, J.C., 1955, Geologic cross sections sponsored by geological societies affiliated or cooperating with the American Association of Petroleum Geologists, 1931-1955: American Association of Petroleum Geologists Bulletin, v. 39, p. 1405-1416.

Malinconico, L.L., Jr., 1987, On the variation of SO_2 emission from volcanoes: Journal of Volcanology and Geothermal Research, v. 33, p. 231-237.

Malone, G.B., 1975, Epithermal gold-silver veins of Central America and SO2 emission from Hawaiian and Italian volcanoes: Hanover, New Hampshire, Dartmouth College, Ph.D dissertation, 100 p.

Malone, G.B., and Stoiber, R.E., 1987, Caldera-related gold mineralization of the El Limón mining district, western Nicaragua: Journal of Volcanology and Geothermal Research, v. 33, p. 217-222.

Mann, P., and Burke, K., 1981, Early Cenozoic evolution of the Caribbean Plate [abs.]: Geological Society of America Abstracts with Programs, v. 13, p. 503.

Mann, P., and Rosencrantz, E., 1988, Fault termination effects of a large-offset transform; integration of marine and onshore data from the western Cayman Trough: Eos (American Geophysical Union, Transactions), v. 69, p. 1449.

Mann, W.P., 1983, Cenozoic tectonics of the Caribbean; structural and stratigraphic studies in Jamaica and Hispaniola: Binghamton, N.Y., State University of New York, Ph.D dissertation, 777 p.

Marin, C.E., Ubeda, G.E., and Viramonte, J., 1973, Contribucion al conocimiento de la genesis del "Talpetate" en Nicaragua [Contribution to the understanding of the genesis of "Talpetate" in Nicaragua]: Publicaciones Geológicas del Instituto Centroamericano Investigación Technología Industrial, v. 4, p. 123-138.

Marshall, W.C., 1930, Nicaragua-its geology and oil possibilities: Oil Bulletin, v. 16, p. 720-724.

Martin, K.P.H.A., 1973, Geology of eastern and central Nicaragua; interpretation of side-looking radar imagery: American Association of Petroleum Geologists Bulletin, v. 57, p. 792.

--- 1974, Application of side-looking radar in earth-resource surveys, in Environmental remote sensing; application and achievements; Rocks, soils, and landforms: New York, N.Y., Crane, Russak & Co., Inc., p. 29-48.

--- 1980, Regional interpretation of radar imagery, in Ackermann, F., ed., Proceedings of the 14th Congress of the International Society for Photogammetry: New York, International Society for Photogammetry, v. 23, p. 624-633, (7 Refs.).

Martin, K.P.H.A., and Williams, A.K., 1974, Radargeologic map of eastern Nicaragua: Memoria de la Novena Conferencia Geologica Inter-Guayanas Publicación Especial, v. 6, p. 600-605.

Martinez, 1971, Investigacion de mineralizaciones económicas en el sector de Achuapa, San Juan de Limay, Leon y Esteli, Nicaragua: Managua, Nicaragua, Servicio Geológico Nacional de Nicaragua, 16 p., (covers Hoja de Achuapa No. 2855).

Martínez, M., and Kuang, J., 1973, Mapa geológico preliminar de Nicaragua: Instituto Geográfico Nacional de Nicaragua Mapa Geológico, scale 1:1,000,000.

Martinez, M., and Viramonte, J., 1973, Estudio geológico de la Cordillera de los Marrabios, Nicaragua [Geology of the Marrabios Range, Nicaragua]: Publicaciones Geológicas del Instituto Centroamericano Investigación Technología Industrial, v. 4, p. 139-147.

Martinez, N.P., 1963, Depósitos aluviales siliceos: Boletín del Servicio Geológico Nacional de Nicaragua, v. 7, p. 51-96.

--- 1974, Rio Negro, Nicaragua: Servicio Geológico Nacional de Nicaragua Mapa Geologico Map 3348-1, scale 1:50,000.

--- 1974, Boca de San Carlos, Nicaragua: Servico Geológico Nacional de Nicaragua Mapa Geológico Map 3348-2, scale 1:50,000.

--- 1974, Cerro Chiripa, Nicaragua: Servico Geológico Nacional de Nicaragua Mapa Geológico Map 3349-1, scale 1:50,000.

--- 1974, San Juan del Norte, Nicaragua: Servico Geológico Nacional de Nicaragua Mapa Geológico Map 3448-1, scale 1:50,000.

--- 1974, Trinidad, Nicaragua: Servico Geológico de Nicaragua Mapa Geológico Map 3448-3, scale 1:50,000.

--- 1974, Laguna Silico, Nicaragua: Servico Geológico Nacional de Nicaragua Mapa Geológico Map 3448-4, scale 1:50,000.

--- 1974, Rio Indio, Nicaragua: Servico Geolóico Nacional de Nicaragua Mapa Geológico Map 3449-3, scale 1:50,000.

--- 1975, Cerro La Guinea, Nicaragua.; Mapa Geologico, Nicaragua; 1:50,000. (3349-2); Sem. Geol. Nac., Managua; Nicaragua.

Martinez, T.E., Arcia, L.R., and Sabatino, G., 1988, Geothermal development in Nicaragua: Geothermics, v. 17, no. 2/3, p. 333-354.

Martini, M., and Giannini, L., 1989, Different roles of water in volcanic phenomena, as derived by the changing chemical compositions of fumarolic gases: Bulletin New Mexico Bureau of Mines and Mineral Resources, p. 177.

Matl, V., 1983, Drahe kameny Nikaraguy [Precious stones of Nicaragua]: Sborník Geologicky Pruzkum Ostrava, v. 27, p. 151-155.

Matsumoto, R., 1987, Nature and occurrence of gas hydrates and their implications to geologic phenomena: Chishitsugaku Zasshi, v. 93, p. 597-615.

Matumoto, T., Ohtake, M., Latham, G., and Umana, J., 1977, Crustal structure in southern Central America: Bulletin Seismological Society of America, v. 67, p. 121-134.

McBirney, A.R., 1955, Aspecto quimico de la actividad de fumarolas en Nicaragua y El Salvador: University of El Salvador, Institute of Tropical Scientific Investigations Communications, v. 3-4, p. 95-100.

--- 1955, Thoughts on the eruption of the Nicaraguan volcano Las Pilas: Bulletin Volcanologique, v. 2, p. 113-117.

--- 1955, The origin of the Nejapa pits near Managua, Nicaragua: Bulletin Volcanologique, v. 2, p. 145-154.

--- 1956, The Nicaraguan volcano Masaya and its caldera: American Geophysical Union Transactions, v. 37, p. 83-96.

--- 1958, Active volcanoes of Nicaragua and Costa Rica; Central America, in Catalogue of the active volcanoes of the world including solfatara fields: Naples, Italy, International Volcanologic Association, v. 6, p. 107-146.

--- 1964, Notas sobre los centros volcanicos cuaternarios al este de la depresion nicaraguense: Boletín del Servicio Geológico Nacional de Nicaragua, v. 8, p. 90-97.

--- 1968, Second additional theory of origin of fiamme in ignimbrites: Nature, v. 217, p. 938.

McBirney, A.R., and Williams, H., 1963, The origin of the Nicaraguan depression: American Geophysical Union Transactions, v. 44, p. 113-114.

--- 1964, The origin of the Nicaraguan depression: Bulletin of Volcanology, v. 27, p. 63.

--- 1965, Volcanic history of Nicaragua: University of California Publications in the Geological Sciences, v. 55, p. 1-65.

McIntyre, D.F., 1961, Summary of geology of La Luz Mines Ltd: La Luz Mines Ltd., * p.

Metal Bulletin, 1982, Nicaragua details gold silver output: Metal Bulletin, v. 6689, p. 15.

Middleton, R.S., and Campbell, E.E., 1979, Geophysical and geochemical methods for mapping gold-bearing structures in Nicaragua, in Hood, J.P., ed., Geophysics and geochemistry in the search for metallic ores: Ontario, Canada, Canadian Geologic Survey, v. 31, p. 779-798.

Milionis, P.N., 1987, Rare earth element geochemistry of lavas from Central America; constraints for basalt petrogenesis: New Brunswick, Rutgers State University, Masters thesis, 105 p.

Miller, B.L., 1941, Investigations at the Siuna Operations of the La Luz Mines Limited: La Luz Mines Ltd., 28 p.

Miller, H.H., 1897, The Segovia gold region of Nicaragua: Engineering and Mining Journal, v. 64, p. 335-336.

Mills, R.A., and Hugh, K.E., 1971, Reconnaissance geologic map of Mosquitia region, Honduras and Nicaragua Caribbean coast, in Transactions of the Caribbean geological conference: v. 5, p. 115.

--- 1974, Reconnaissance Geologic Map of Mosquitia Region, Honduras and Nicaragua Caribbean Coast: American Association of Petroleum Geologists Bulletin, v. 58, p. 189-207.

Mining Annual Review, 1978, Central America: Mining Annual Review, v. 1978, p. 399.

Moore, J.L., Osbun, E., and Storm, P., V, 1981, Geology and temperature distribution of Momotombo geothermal field, Nicaragua: American Association of Petroleum Geologists Studies in Geology, v. 12, p. 33-54.

Moore, J.L., Jr., Storm, P.V., Ferrey, C., and Osbun, E., 1978, Geology and development of Momotombo geothermal field, Nicaragua: American Association of Petroleum Geologists Bulletin, v. 62, p. 1229.

Morales, A., 1988, Fluid inclusion studies of gold-bearing quartz veins in La Libertad mining district, Nicaragua: Stockholm, University of Stockholm, Bachelors thesis, 34 p.

Moreno, A.M., and Casteel, K.D., 1986, Latin American gold mining; a growing force in the world market, in Smale-Adams, K.B., ed., Papers presented at the Mining Latin America/Mineria Latinoamericana Conference: London, England, Institute of Mining and Metallurgy, p. 285-297.

Moreno, H., 1982, Reservas de Mineral del Tajo Abierto, Cerro Potosi: Corporacion Nicaraguense de Desarrollo Minero, 6 p.

--- 1982, Proyecto de Esploración Geológica, Area de Mina Siuna:, * p.

Mullerried, F.K.G., 1948, Las facies de fauna y flora del Mesozoico en el noroeste de la America central (del Istmo de Tehuantepec a Nicaragua), in Titles and Abstracts for the International Geological Congress: London, England, p. 71.

--- 1949, Rectificación de la estratigrafía del Mesozoico en el noroeste de America Central (del Istmo de Tehuantepec a Nicaragua): Ciencia, v. 9, p. 219-223.

--- 1952, Las facies de fauna y flora del Mesozoico en el noroeste de la America Central (del istmo de Tehuantepec a Nicaragua): London, England, International Geological Congress, 73 p.

Narskikh, R.S., 1973, Yuzhnaya i Tsentral'naya Amerika [South and Central America], in Regional'naya kharakteristika obzornykh gormorfologicheskikh kart sushi [regional characterization of general geomorphologic maps of land]: Moscow, Izd. Nauka, Geomorfologicheskoye Kartovedeniye SSSR i chastey sveta, p. 174-202.

Nelson, G.A., 1948, The geology of the La Luz Mines Limited and Northeastern Nicaragua: La Luz Mines Ltd., * p.

Nelson, G.A., and Spencer, C.L., 1952, The geology of La Luz mines, Ltd., Siuna, Nicaragua: Mines Magazine, v. 42, p. 37-38.

Neptune Mining Co., 1979, Ore Reserves, December 1, 1979: Managua, Nicaragua, Instituto Nicaraguense de la Mineria, * p.

--- 1979, Ore Reserves, inactive mines, December 1, 1979: Managua, Nicaragua, Neptune Mining Company, * p.

Nwaochei, B.N., 1981, Geophysical investigations of the Nicaraguan Rise: New Brunswick, Rutgers State University, Ph.D. dissertation, 87 p.

Nyström, J.O., Levi, B., Troeng.B, Ehrenborg, J., and Carranza, G., 1988, geochemistry of volcanic rocks in a geotraverse through Nicaragua: Revista Geologica de America Central, v. 8, p. 77-109.

Okita, T., and Shimozuru, D., 1974, Remote sensing of volcanic gases; Amount of sulfur dioxide emitted from volcanoes: Bulletin of the Volcanology Society of Japan, v. 19, p. 63-64.

Ortega, A., Bermúdez, F., Dornan, J., Swartling, A., Pettersson, L.O., and Ekstrand, B., 1989, Evaluación del potencial para el desarrollo productivo en la Empresa Minera Siuna: Instituto Nicaraquense de la Mineria and Sverges Geologiska A.B., 23 p.

Page, W.D., 1978, The geology of the El Bosque archaeological site, Nicaragua, in Bryan, A.L., ed., Early man in America; from a circum-Pacific perspective: Alberta, Canada, University of Alberta, v. 1, p. 231-260.

Pan American Institute of Geography and History, 1953, Estudio preliminar en Guatemala, El Salvador, Honduras, Nicaragua, Costa Rica, Panama y Zona del Canal: Mexico, D.F., Pan American Institute of Geography and History, Los estudios sobre los recuroso naturales en las Americas, v. 1, 446 p.

Pan American Union, 1965, Nicaragua--Annotated index of aerial photographic coverage and mapping of topography and natural resources: Washington, D.C., Pan American Union, Department of Economic Affairs, 13 p.

Parsons, J.J., 1955, Gold Mining in the Nicaragua Rain Forest, in Yearbook of the Association of Pacific Coast Geographers: Berkeley, California, University of California, p. 49-55.

Parsons, W.H., 1970, Current status of Central American volcanoes: Eos (American Geophysical Union, Transactions), v. 51, p. 440.

--- 1970, Cerro Negro volcano: American Association of Petroleum Geologists Explorer, v. 12, p. 16-19.

Parsons Corporation, 1972, The geology of western Nicaragua: Managua, Nicaragua tax improvement and natural resources inventory project, Final Technical Report, v. IV, 220 p.

Patterson, J.A., Stoiber, R.E., Williams, S.N., and Abiko, T., 1983, The systematics of fumarolic mineral incrustations at Momotombo Volcano, Nicaragua, and Usu Volcano, Japan: Eos (American Geophysical Union, Transactions), v. 64, p. 892.

Paz, R.N., 1962, Reconocimiento geológico en la cuenca hidrografica de los rios Coco y Bocay: Boletín del Servicio Geológico Nacional de Nicaragua, v. 6, p. 5-22.

--- 1964, Reconocimiento geologico de la costa del Pacifico de Nicaragua: Boletín del Servicio Geológico Nacional de Nicaragua, v. 8, p. 69-87.

--- 1965, Informe preliminar sobre un reconocimiento geologico en la costa del Pacifico de Nicaragua: Boletín de Asociacíon Mexicana Geólogos Petroleros, v. 17, p. 17-27.

Perfit, M.R., and Heezen, B.C., 1978, The geology and evolution of the Cayman Trench: Geological Society of America Bulletin, v. 89, p. 1155-1174.

Pineiro, R.F., and Romero, R.S., 1962, Reconocimiento geológico minero de la porcion noroeste de la Republica de Nicaragua, A.C: Boletín del Servicio Geológico Nacional de Nicaragua, v. 6, p. 50-90.

Plecash, J., and Hopper, R.V., 1962, Reporte de las minas La Luz y Rosita: Corporacíon Nicaraguense de Minas, p. *.

Plecash, J., Hopper, R.V., et al., 1963, Operations at La Luz mines and Rosita mines, Nicaragua, Central America: Canadian Mining and Metallurgical Bulletin, v. 56, p. 624-641.

Pushcharovskiy, Y.M., 1979, Problemy tektoniki i geodinamiki Karibskogo regiona [Problems of tectonics and geodynamics of the Caribbean region], in Pushcharovskiy, Y.M., Lomize, M.G., and Ryabukhin, A.G., eds., Tektonika i geodinamika Karibskogo regiona [Tectonics and geodynamics of the Caribbean region]: Moscow, USSR, Izd. Nauk, p. 7-12, (16 Refs).

Pushkar, P., McBirney, A.R., and Kudo, A.M., 1972, The isotopic composition of strontium in central American ingimbrites: Bulletin of Volcanology, v. 35, p. 265-294.

Quisefit, J.P., Toutain, J.P., Bergametti, G., Javoy, M., Cheynet, B., and Person, A., 1989, Evolution versus cooling of gaseous volcanic emissions from Momotombo Volcano, Nicaragua; thermochemical model and observations: Geochimica et Cosmochimica Acta, v. 53, p. 2591-2608.

Quisefit, J.P., Toutain, J.P., and Mouvier, G., 1988, On a thermodynamical model adopted for the condensation of gaseous volcanic emissions: Chemical Geology, v. 70, p. 155.

Ransome, F.L., 1899, Microscopic petrography of the rocks from the Nicaragua Canal region, in Nicaragua Canal Commission: Baltimore, U.S. Nicaraguan Canal Commission, Report 1897-1899, p. 184-192.

Reed, M.J., 1977, Geochemical comparison of deep geothermal waters in North America [abs.]: Geological Society of America Abstracts with Programs, v. 9, p. 1138.

Reeside, J.B., Jr., 1957, Correlation of the Triassic formations of North America, exclusive of Canada: Geological Society of America Bulletin, v. 68, p. 1451-1513.

Reyes, R., Padilla, B., Rojas, R., and Godoy, M., 1990, Diseño para una prueba de lixiviación por montón con capacidad de 3,300 t/mensuales para el material de los relaves auriferos, empresa minera Siuna, Nicaragua: Corporacíon Nicaraguense de Minas, p. *.

Rezak, R., Antoine, J.W., Bryant, W.R., Fahlquist, D.A., and Bouma, A.H., 1972, Preliminary results of Cruise 71-A-4 of the R/V Alaminos in the Caribbean, in Transactions of the Caribbean Geological Conference: Caribbean Geological conference, v. 6, p. 441-449.

Ritchie, A.W., and Finch, R.C., 1984, Guayape fault system of Honduras [abs.]: Geological Society of America Abstracts with Programs, v. 16, p. 635.

--- 1985, Widespread Jurassic strata on the Chortis Block of the Caribbean Plate [abs.]: Geological Society of America Abstracts with Programs, v. 17, p. 700-701.

Rivera, A., 1976, Feasibility study to redesign the Rosita open pit, Tunky District, Zelaya State, Republic of Nicaragua: Publicaciones Geológicas del Instituto Centroamericano Investigación Technología Industrial, p. 241-246.

--- 1979, Siuna open-pit ore reserves, Summary (solo una tabla): Rosario Mining of Nicaragua, Inc., * p.

Rivier, F., 1973, Contribucion estratigráfica sobre la geológia de La Cuenca de Limón, zona de Turrialba, Costa Rica [Stratigraphy of the Limon Basin, near Turrialba, Costa Rica]: Publicaciones Geológicas del Instituto Centroamericano Investigación Technología Industrial, v. 4, p. 149-159.

Roberts, R.J., and Irving, E.M., 1957, Mineral deposits of Central America: U.S. Geological Survey, Bulletin 1034, 205 p., 16 plates.

Robinson, E., 1988 [1989], Age and distribution of the Chapelton Formation, Nicaragua Rise: Journal of the Geological Society of Jamaica, v. 25, p. 42.

Rodriguez, B.D., 1976, The teaching of photo-interpretation and photogrammetry in the field of natural resources in Central America and Mexico, in Proceedings of the American Society of Photogammetry: American Society of Photogammetry, Technical Paper No. 75-259, v. 42, p. 430-442.

--- 1977, The teaching of photo-interpretation and photogrammetry in the field of natural resources: Photogrammetric Engineering and Remote Sensing, v. 43, p. 285-291.

Rodriguez, M.O., Price, V.B., Hodgson, V.G., Valle, G.C., and Ubeda, G.E., 1976, Resumen de las labores realizadas por el Servicio Geologico Nacional desde el 1ro. de julio 1956 hasta el mes de abril 1976 [Summary of the research done by the National Geological Survey from July 1, 1956 until April, 1976]: Managua, Nicaragua, Servicio Geológico Nacional, .

Romero, S.J., 1984, Sistema racional de drenaje de las aguas termales en el yacimiento aurifero Santa Pancha, Nicaragua [Rational drainage system for thermal waters of the auriferous deposit of Santa Pancha, Nicaragua] [abs.], in Bogdanov, N.A.T., ed., Abstracts of the 27th International Geological Congress: International Geological Congress, v. 7, p. 502.

Rubel, D.N., 1972, Major-element distribution within the olivines of the 1971 Cerro Negro volcano ash-cloud eruption [abs.]: Geological Society of America Abstracts with Programs, v. 4, p. 348.

Rudolph, J.D., 1982, Nicaragua; a country study: Washington, D. C., American University foreign area studies, (2nd ed.) Area handbook series, 53 p.

Rybach, L., 1985, Heat flow and geothermal processes: Journal of Geodynamics, v. 4, p. 1-4.

Sapper, K.T., 1937, Mittelamerika (unter Mitarbeit von Walther Staub) [Middle America]: Heidelberg, Carl Winter, Handbuch der regionalen Geologie 4, v. 8, 160 p., (Heft 29).

Schmidt, H., and Winsemann, J., 1988, Depositional sequences in the convergent plate margin setting of the southern Central American island arc: Memori Canadian Society of Petroleum Geologists, v. 15, p. 583.

Schuster, G.T., 1977, Seismic studies of crustal structure in Nicaragua and Costa Rica: Houston, University of Houston, Masters thesis, 75 p.

Schwartz, D.P., Packer, D.R., and Weaver, K.D., 1975, New information on offset of the Central American volcanic chain near Managua, Nicaragua [abs.]: Geological Society of America Abstracts with Programs, v. 7, p. 1262.

Scobey, J., 1920, The La Luz and Los Angeles Mine in Nicaragua: Engineering and Mining Journal, v. 110, p. 6-13.

Scrutton, M.E., and Escalante, G.F., 1986, Petroleum geology of Pacific margin of Central America and northern South America, from Guatemala to Ecuador: American Association of Petroleum Geologists Bulletin, v. 70, p. 934.

Servicio Geodetico Interamericano, 1973, Estudios de los patrones de daños sismicos por medio de fotointerpretacion [Studies of the seismic damage patterns through photointerpretation], in First Pan American symposium on remote sensing: Panamá City, Panamá, Servicio Geodetico Interamericano, p. 298-308.

Servicio Geológico Nacional, 1975, Rio Sabalos, Nicaragua: Servicio Geológico Nacional, Managua, Nicaragua Geológico Map 3349-4, scale 1:50,000.

Seyfried, H., Astorga, G.A., Calvo, C., and Laurito, C., 1987, Sequence response (cyclicity, biostratinomy, ichnofacies) to subsidence, sea level fluctuations, and exceptional events in Cenozoic fore arc basins of southern Central America, in McNulty, C.L., and Waterman, A.S., eds., Innovative biostratigraphic approaches to sequence analysis; new exploration opportunities: Arlington, Texas, University of Texas, p. 31-51.

Shor, G.G., Jr., 1974, Continental margin of Middle America, in Burk, C.A., and Drake, C.L., eds., The geology of continental margins: New York, N.Y., Springer-Verlag, p. 599-602.

Sisselman, R., 1986, Prospección de recursos minerales via satélite; un enfoque para la tele-exploración [Mineral resource exploration via satellite; a focus for tele-exploration]: De Re Metallica, v. 15-16, p. 4-11.

Smit, W., 1967, Project Vesubio: Neptune Mining Co., 14 p.

Snell, J.D., 1966, Vesubio lead-zinc project, Geologic Report: Managua, Nicaragua, Neptune Mining Company, 44 p.

Soldan, J., 1982, Geologie a nerostne suroviny Nikaraguy [Geology and raw materials of Nicaragua]: Geologicky Pruzkum, v. 24, p. 351-354.

Solorzano, M.R., 1960, Analisis y perspectivas industriales de los recursos minerales de Nicaragua: Boletín del Servicio Geológico Nacional de Nicaragua, v. 4, p. 119-161.

Spassov, V., Fredrikdon, G., Dominguez, A., Rios, D., Moore, F., Castellón, R., Alvarez, A., Sinclari, A., Coleman, G., and Ramirez, O., 1990, Informe preliminar sobre las reservas activas del Distrito Minero de Bonanza: Corporación Nicaraguense de Minas, p. 4.

Spassov, V., Fredrikson, G., Dominquez, A., Rios, D., Moore, F., Castellón, R., Sinclair, A., Coleman, G., and Ramirez, O., 1990, Informe preliminar sobre las reservas activas del Distrito Minero de Bonanza: Managua, Nicaragua, Instituto Nicaraguense de la Mineria, 4 p.

Stoiber, R.E., and Carr, M.J., 1973, Quaternary volcanic and tectonic segmentation of Central America: Bulletin of Volcanology, v. 37, p. 304-325.

Stoiber, R.E., Malone, G.B., and Bratton, G.P., 1978, Volcanic emission of SO2 at Italian and Central American volcanoes [abs.]: Geological Society of America Abstracts with Programs, v. 10, p. 148.

Stoiber, R.E., and Rose, W.I., Jr., 1974, Fumarole incrustations at active Central American volcanoes: Geochimica et Cosmochimica Acta, v. 38, p. 495-516.

Stoiber, R.E., and Wiliams, S.N., 1984, A collaborative geochemical monitoring program of volcanoes in Nicaragua and Costa Rica: International Geological Congress, v. 27, p. 408.

Stoiber, R.E., Williams, S.N., and Huebert, B.J., 1982, Emission of Hg degrees and Rn from Nicaraguan and Costa Rican volcanoes: Eos (American Geophysical Union, Transactions), v. 63, p. 1152.

--- 1984, Geochemical changes during non-eruptive degassing of basaltic magma at Masaya Caldera complex, Nicaragua [abs.]: Geological Society of America Abstracts with Programs, v. 16, p. 669-670.

--- 1986, Sulfur and halogen gases at Masaya Caldera complex, Nicaragua; total flux and variations with time, in Sato, Motoaki, Matsuo, S., King, and Chi-Yu, eds., Gas geochemistry of volcanism, earthquakes, resource exploration, Earth's interior: U.S. Geological Survey Special Paper, p. 91.

Stonehouse, J.M., 1976, Movement of mineralizing fluids, Bonanza Mining District, Nicaragua: Dartmouth College, Hanover, New Hampshire, Masters thesis, 63 p.

Stringham, J.R., 1967, Mining methods, Vesubio Project: Neptune Mining Company, 7 p.

Stroiber, R.E., 1982, Sulfur dioxide and other gas emission from Masaya Volcano, Nicaragua: Boletin de Vulcanología, v. 6, p. 49-51.

Sundblad, K., Cumming, G.L., and Krstic, D., 1991, Lead isotope evidence for the formation of epithermal gold quartz veins in the Chortis Block, Nicaragua: Economic Geology, v. 86, p. 944-959.

Sussman, D., 1982, Pyroclastic geology of Apoyo Caldera, Nicaragua: Eos (American Geophysical Union, Transactions), v. 63, p. 1155.

--- 1985, Apoyo Caldera, Nicaragua; a major Quaternary silicic eruptive center: Journal of Volcanology and Geothermal Research, v. 24, p. 249-282.

Swartling, A., 1989, Análisis de costos de requisitos de ley oz/tc en Bonanza: Corporacíon Nicaraguense de Minas, v. 89011, p. 8.

Sykes, L.R., McCann, W.R., and Kafka, A.L., 1982, Motion of the Caribbean plate during last 7 million years and implications for earlier Cenozoic movements: Journal of Geophysical Research B, v. 87, p. 10656-10676.

Teran, F., and Incer, B.J., 1964, Geografía de Nicaragua: Managua, Nicaragua, Banco Central de Nicaragua, (1st ed.) 266 p.

Tomblin, J.F., 1977, Caribbean seismicity, in Weaver, J.D., ed., Geology, geophysics and resources of the Caribbean; report of the IDOE Workshop on the geology and marine geophysics of the Caribbean region and its resources: New York, United Nations Educational, Scientific, and Cultural Organization, p. 63-77.

Tonani, F.B., and Teilman, M.A., 1980, Geochemistry at Momotombo, Nicaragua; one aspect in a geothermal field case history: Transactions of the Geothermal Resources Council, v. 4, p. 193-196.

Trejos M, S., 1982, Informe sobre la planta de beneficio de Siuna: Corporacíon Nicaraguense de Minas, p. *.

Triffleman, N.J., Hallock, P., and Hine, A.C., 1987, Morphology, sediments, and depositional environments of a partially drowned carbonate platform; Serranilla Bank, Southwest Caribbean Sea [abs.]: Geological Society of America Abstracts with Programs, v. 19, p. 871.

Troeng, B., and Hodgson, V.G., 1985, The Nicaraguan geotraverse; a multidisciplinary study: Memorias Congreso Latinoamericano de Geología, v. 6, p. 36-45.

Twenhofel, W.H., 1954, Correlation of the Ordovician formations of North America: Geological Society of America Bulletin, v. 65, p. 247-298.

Urrutia S, A., 1985, Informe General sobre Cálculo de Reservas Minerales en Siuna: Corporacion Nicaraguense de Desarrollo Minero, p. 6.

Valyashko, G.M., Yel'tsina, G.N., Litvin, V.M., Rudenko, M.V., Ryabukhin, A.G., Savostin, L.A., and Khain, V.Y., 1975, Geologo-geofizicheskaya kharakteristika osnovnykh strukturnykh elementov Meksikano-Karibskogo regiona [Geologic-geophysical features of the main structures in the Mexican-Caribbean region], in Rass, T.S., ed., Kompleksnyye issledovaniya Karibskogo morya, Meksikanskogo Zaliva i sopredel'nykh: Moscow, Zavod Akademii Nauk SSSR, Instituta Okeanologija Trudy, v. 100, p. 54-68.

Velasco, H.J., 1964, Estudio geoeléctrico en el trayecto de los canales "Del Lago" y "Del Brujo" empresa de riego de Rwalkerivas [geoelectric study in the canal sections of the "Lago" and "Brujo" irrigation project in Rivas]: Boletín del Servicio Geológico Nacional de Nicaragua, v. 8, p. 99-108.

Venable, M., and Darce, M., 1990, Propuesta de Prospeccion Geológica para el Distrito Minero de Siuna: Corporacíon Nicaraguense de Minas, p. 15.

Victor, L., 1976, Structures of the continental margin of Central America from northern Nicaragua to northern Panama: Corvallis, Oregon State University, Masters thesis, 97 p.

Victor, L.S., and Couch, R., 1975, Structure of the continental margin of Nicaragua and Costa Rica: Eos (American Geophysical Union, Transactions), v. 56, p. 1065.

Viramonte, J., and Williams, R.L., 1973, Estudio preliminar sobre las ignimbritas andesiticas de Nicaragua [Preliminary study of the andesitic ignimbrites of Nicaragua]: Publicaciones Geológicas del Instituto Centroamericano Investigación Technología Industrial, v. 4, p. 171-177.

Viramonte, J.G., and Discala, L., 1970, Summary of the 1968 eruption of Cerro Negro, Nicaragua: Bulletin Volcanologique, v. 34, p. 347-351.

Viramonte, J.G., Ubeda, E., and Martinez, M., 1971, The 1971 eruption of Cerro Negro, Nicaragua: Washington, D.C., Smithsonian Institute Center of Short-Lived Phenomenon, 28 p.

Wadge, G., and Wooden, J.L., 1982, Late Cenozoic alkaline volcanism in the northwestern Caribbean; tectonic setting and Sr isotopic characteristics: Earth and Planetary Science Letters, v. 57, p. 35-46.

Walker, J.A., 1981, Petrogenesis of lavas from cinder cone fields behind the volcanic front of Central America: Journal of Geology, v. 89, p. 721-739.

--- 1982, Basalts from lines of cinder cones on the volcanic front in Nicaragua, Central America: Eos (American Geophysical Union, Transactions), v. 63, p. 452.

--- 1982, Volcanic rocks from Nejapa and Granada cinder cone alignments, Nicaragua, Central America: New Brunswick, Rutgers State University, Ph.D dissertation, 155 p.

--- 1984, Volcanic rocks from the Nejapa and Granada cinder cone alignments, Nicaragua, Central America: Journal of Petrology, v. 25, p. 299-342.

Walker, J.A., and Carr, M.J., 1986, Compositional variations caused by phenocryst sorting at Cerro Negro Volcano, Nicaragua: Geological Society of America Bulletin, v. 97, p. 1156-1162.

Walker, J.A., and Williams, S.N., 1986, Shallow magmatic processes beneath Masaya Caldera Complex, Nicaragua: Eos (American Geophysical Union, Transactions), v. 67, p. 411.

Ward, P.L., Eaton, J.P., Endo, E., Harlow, D., Marquez, D., and Allen, R., 1973, Establishment, test, and evaluation of a prototype volcano-surveillance system, in Proceedings of the Symposium on significant results obtained form the Earth Resources Technology Satellite-1: Washington, D.C., National Aeronautics and Space Administration, Special Publication Section A, 327, v. 1, p. 305-315.

Weber, H.D., and Wiesemann, G., 1978, Mapa geológico de la República de El Salvador, América Central: Bundesanstalt Geowisschaft Rohstoffe, Berlin Geologic, scale 1:100,000.

Wegemann, C.H., 1931, Geology of southern Nicaragua: Geological Society of America Bulletin, v. 42, p. 194, also in Pan-Am Geologist v. 55, no. 1, pp. 67-68.

West, H.E., 1909, Features of a vein formation in Nicaragua: Engineering and Mining Journal, v. 87, p. 1130-1133.

Weyl, R., 1961, Die Geologie Mittelamerikas [The geology of Middle America]: Berlin, Gebruder Borntraeger, Beitrage zur regionalen Geologie der Erde, v. 1, 226 p.

--- 1966, Orogenesis in Central America, in Transactions of the Caribbean Geological Conference: Kingston, Jamacian Geological Survey, Special Publication, p. 91-94.

--- 1970, Geologische bilder aus Mittelamerika [Geologic illustrations from Central America], in Den ignimbritplateaus von Honduras und Nicaragua [The ignimbrite plateaus of Honduras and Nicaragua]: Frankfurt, Natur und Museum (Senckenbergische Naturforschende Gesellschaft), v. 100, pt 5., p. 362-370.

--- 1980, Geology of Central America: Berlin, Gebrueder Borntraeger, (2nd ed.) Beitraege zur regionalen Beologie der Erde, v. 15, 226 p., 600 refs.

Weyl, R., and Pichler, H., 1973, Petrochemical aspects of Central American magmatism: Publicaciones Geológicas del Instituto Centroamericano Investigación Technología Industrial, v. 4, p. 81-90.

Widenfalk, L., and Altamirano, G., 1985, Distribution of main and trace elements at the Panteón Vein, La Pancha, El Limón, Nicaragua: Luleå, Sweden, Sverges Geologiska A.B., 56 p.

Wilber, R.J., 1987, Albatross, Pedro, Alice, Rosalind and No-Name; the current-shaped carbonate banks of the Nicaraguan Rise [abs.]: Society of Economic Paleontologists and Mineralogists Abstracts, v. 4, p. 91-92.

Williams, S.N., 1982, Basaltic ignimbrite erupted from Masaya Caldera complex, Nicaragua: Eos (American Geophysical Union, Transactions), v. 63, p. 1155.

--- 1983, Geology and eruptive mechanisms of Masaya Caldera complex, Nicaragua: Hanover, New Hampshire, Dartmouth College, Ph.D dissertation, 216 p.

Williams, S.N., and Stoiber, R.E., 1983, "Masaya-type caldera"; redefined as the mafic analogue of the "krakatau-type Caldera": Eos (American Geophysical Union, Transactions), v. 64, p. 877.

Wilson, H.H., 1974, Cretaceous sedimentation and orogeny in Nuclear Central America: American Association of Petroleum Geologists Bulletin, v. 58, p. 1348-1396.

Winsemann, J., 1986, Faziesassoziationen hemipelagischer Ablagerungen im Bereich der suedlichen Mittelamerikanischen Landbruecke [Facies associations in hemipelagic environments in the area of the southern Central America land bridge]: Berliner Geowissenchaftliche Abhandlungen Reihe A: Geologie und Palaeontologie, v. Sonderband, p. 74.

Woodring, W.P., 1960, The Oligocene and Miocene in the Caribbean region, in Transactions of the second Caribbean Geological Conference Mayaguez, Puerto Rico: Mayaguez, Puerto Rico, Caribbean Geological Conference, p. 27-32.

--- 1976, Age of El Salto Formation of Nicaragua: Publicaciones Geológicas del Instituto Centroamericano Investigación Technología Industrial, v. 5, p. 18-21.

--- 1977 [1978], Distribution of Tertiary marine molluscan faunas in southern Central America and northern South America, in Ferrusquia-Villafranca, I., ed., Proceedings of the simposio interdisciplinario sobre paleogeografia Mesoamericana: Mexico City, Universidad Nacional Autonomis de Mexico, Boletin del Instituto Geológico 101, p. 153-165.

Zamora, M., and Darce, M., 1991, Informacion sobre el mineral de hierro en la República de Nicaragua: Corporacíon Nicaraguense de Minas, p. 7.

Zoppis, B.L., 1957, Estudio geológico de la region de Palacagüina y de su depósito de antimonio: Boletín del Servicio Geológico Nacional de Nicaragua, v. 1, p. 29-34.

--- 1959, Resumen de una investigacion geoelectrica para agua en la region de Potosi: Boletín del Servicio Geológico Nacional de Nicaragua, v. 3, p. 23-27.

--- 1959, Los depositos de yeso de Santa Rosa del Peñon: Boletín del Servicio Geológico Nacional de Nicaragua, v. 3, p. 89-109.

--- 1960, Viejas minas de plata en Macuelizo: Boletín del Servicio Geológico Nacional de Nicaragua, p. 39-59.

--- 1960, Reconocimiento geológico-minero para el fosfato en el Departamento de Rivas: Boletín del Servicio Geológico Nacional de Nicaragua, v. 4, p. 85-117.

--- 1961, Estudio preliminar de las mineralizaciones de tungsteno y molíbdeno de Macuelizo, Departamento de Nueva Segovia: Boletín del Servicio Geológico Nacional de Nicaragua, p. 31-51.

Zoppis, B.L., and Del Giudice, D., 1960, Reconocimiento geologico del Valle de Punta Gorda: Boletín del Servicio Geológico Nacional de Nicaragua, v. 4, p. 61-83.

Zoppis, B.L., and del Giudice, D., 1957, Relacion sobre las manifestaciones manganesiferas de Terrabona y de Matagalpa: Boletín del Servicio Geológico Nacional de Nicaragua, v. 1, p. 39-41.

--- 1957, Arenisca ferrífera de la formación "El Fraile", Puerto Somoza: Boletín del Servicio Geológico Nacional de Nicaragua, v. 1, p. 43-44.

--- 1958, Geológia de la Costa del Pacifico de Nicaragua: Boletín del Servicio Geológico Nacional de Nicaragua, v. 2, p. 19-68.

--- 1958, Un reconocimiento geológico del Rio Bocay y parte del Rio Coco: Boletín del Servicio Geológico Nacional de Nicaragua, v. 2, p. 81-112.

Zoppis, de S.R., 1956, Informe general sobre los estudios geológico-mineros efectuados durante el ano 1955-1956: Managua, Nicaragua, Nicaragua Servivio Geológico Nacional, 109 p.

--- 1957, Informe sobre el yacimiento de hierro de Monte Carmelo, Departamento de Zelaya, Republica de Nicaragua: Boletín del Servicio Geológico Nacional de Nicaragua, v. 1, p. 13-27.

--- 1957, Informe sobre la arcilla de Jiloa, Managua: Boletín del Servicio Geológico Nacional de Nicaragua, v. 1, p. 77-80.

--- 1957, Marmoles y piedras duras de Nicaragua: Boletín del Servicio Geológico Nacional de Nicaragua, v. 1, p. 81-83.

--- 1958, Posibilidades petroliferas en los departamentos costeros del Pacifico de Nicaragua: Boletín del Servicio Geológico Nacional de Nicaragua, v. 2, p. 71-79.

Zuniga, A., and Lopez, C., 1977, Development of geothermal resources of Nicaragua: Geothermal Energy, v. 5, p. 8-13.

CPSIA information can be obtained at www.ICGtesting.com
Printed in the USA
BVOW06s2343101013

333489BV00007B/65/P